EDITOR: MARTIN WIN... S0-AES-981

OSPREY MILITARY

MEN-AT-ARMS SERIES · 191

HENRY VIII'S ARMY

Text by
PAUL CORNISH
Colour plates by
ANGUS McBRIDE

First published in Great Britain in 1987 by
Osprey, an imprint of Reed Consumer Books Ltd.
Michelin House, 81 Fulham Road,
London SW3 6RB
and Auckland, Melbourne, Singapore and Toronto

© Copyright 1987 Reed International Books Ltd.
Reprinted 1988, 1991, 1992, 1995

British Library Cataloguing in Publication Data

Cornish, Paul
    Henry VIII's army.—(Men-at-arms series;
    191).
    1. England and Wales. *Army*—History
    2. Great Britain—History, Military—
    Tudors, 1485–1603
    I. Title   II. Series
    355'.00941   UA649

ISBN 0 85045 798 X

Filmset in Great Britain
Printed through Bookbuilders Ltd, Hong Kong

Dedication
For Jennifer

Acknowledgements
Special thanks to Gerry Embleton,
Andrew Clary and Chris Gravett.

Artist's Note
Readers may care to note that the original paintings
from which the colour plates in this book were
prepared are available for private sale. All
reproduction copyright whatsoever is retained by the
publisher. All enquiries should be addressed to:
    Scorpio Gallery
    P.O. Box 475
    Hailsham
    E. Sussex BN27 2SL

The publishers regret that they can enter into no
correspondence upon this matter.

If you would like to receive more information about
Osprey Military books, The Osprey Messenger is a
regular newsletter which contains articles, new title
information and special offers. To join free of charge
please write to:

**Osprey Military Messenger,
PO Box 5, Rushden,
Northants NN10 6YX**

Campaigns and Battles

Few eras of British military history have been so neglected as the reign of Henry VIII. Folklore has given us the image of the 'Bluff King Hal' and his six wives, his reputation only slightly tarnished by his predilection for beheading people. Meanwhile, mainstream historians have largely characterised the period as one of religious, social and governmental change. Nevertheless, military affairs occupied a very significant place during Henry VIII's reign. Consequently, the study of his army can reveal much about the period as a whole.

This book is principally concerned with the uniforms and equipment of that army: how they differed from those of their continental neighbours, and how and why they changed and developed. Recruitment and organisation are also discussed, but to put these matters into context it is necessary first to look at the history of Henry VIII's martial endeavours.

* * *

Henry VIII, circa 1520: a corrective to the traditional image of Henry as a corpulent, middle-aged man, this portrait, by an unknown artist, shows him in his prime. (**National Portrait Gallery**)

During Henry VIII's reign English armies saw action against two main enemies: the French and the Scots. France was undoubtedly viewed as the principal foe. Henry nursed grandiose ambitions to be acclaimed as the arbiter of European politics. Intervention in European affairs did not necessarily dictate a policy of hostility towards France; nevertheless, despite certain diplomatic overtures and negotiations, England was invariably to be found in league with France's enemies in time of war. Indeed, such alliances were essential if Henry was to attack France, for she was no longer the weak and divided opponent who once faced Edward III and Henry V.

The French, in their turn, could generally invoke the aid of Scotland against England. The conflict between England and Scotland has tended to overshadow Henry VIII's continental ventures in modern times, though to most contemporaries, it appeared as little more than an adjunct to the conflict with France.

Early Expeditions

In 1511 King Henry made his first forays into Europe. A force of 1,500 archers was sent to the Low Countries, where they met with much success while aiding Margaret of Savoy against the rebellious Duke of Guelders. A larger venture was undertaken

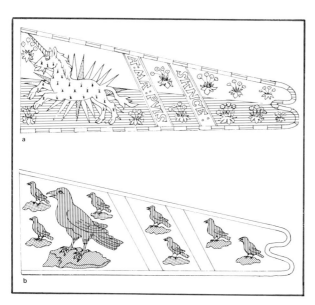

Standards: *(a) The Marquis of Dorset.* **Ground: white and mulberry purple. Unicorn: ermine, with gold and silver rays. The flowers are sprigs of Pinks (white with pink edges).** *(b) Sir Rees Ap Thomas.* **Ground: white. The eight black ravens stand on green mounds. Motto: unknown. Both standards would have borne the cross of St George at the hoist.**

in alliance with Henry's father-in-law, Ferdinand of Aragon. Ferdinand offered what appeared to be a chance to recover erstwhile English possessions in south-western France, and accordingly 5,000 infantry, under the Marquis of Dorset, were despatched to north-eastern Spain. The Spanish were to provide cavalry and logistical support; but Ferdinand was more interested in swallowing-up the independent Spanish kingdom of Navarre than in furthering English aims. Consequently, by the time he finally declared himself ready to invade Guienne the English force, which had provided a convenient shield for his flank, was riddled with disease and indiscipline. All that the English commanders could do was to ship the rump of their army home and face the wrath of the king.

This fiasco did nothing to dampen Henry's warlike ardour. During 1512 plans were laid for the following year; the King, as a member of the Pope's 'Holy League', would personally lead an invasion of northern France.

The Battle of the Spurs
On 30 June 1513 Henry VIII stepped ashore at Calais, having been preceded by an army numbering between 24,000 and 35,000 men—probably the finest English army of the 16th century. Contemporary commentators—including the French—had little but praise for the way in which it conducted itself; and the king's presence obviously enhanced morale and discipline. Unfortunately, the quality of the army was not matched by the quality of its strategic direction, and the objectives pursued probably owed more to Henry's subtle ally, the Emperor Maximilian I, than to English interests.

Firstly, the well-fortified town of Thérouanne was invested by the vanguard and rearguard of the English army; but prior to the arrival of the king with the remainder of the army the siege lines were not drawn tight enough to prevent French infiltration. It was this failing which engendered the only open engagement of the campaign.

On 16 August the French put into operation a plan which they hoped would enable a company of light cavalry to carry powder and provisions to the walls of the beleaguered town. While a diversionary attack was mounted from the north-west, the revictualling force was to try its luck from the south, supported by heavy cavalry—possibly numbering as many as 2,000. Unfortunately for the French, Henry VIII, accompanied by the Emperor, had just moved south of Thérouanne with the main body of his army. The French heavy cavalry thus found themselves facing over 1,000 horse, with at least 10–12,000 infantry following a mile behind. Henry, probably at Maximilian's suggestion, sent forward longbowmen on horseback to engage the French flank from behind a hedge, supported by the fire of light guns. La Palice, the experienced French commander, saw no alternative but to withdraw, whereupon the English horse charged, catching the French as they were about to move off. This disaster for the French was compounded by the arrival of their light cavalry, returning in rout from their vain mission. The entire French force was soon in headlong flight, with the English cavalry in joyful pursuit, accompanied by some men-at-arms lent by the Emperor—thus giving the battle its popular name.

The Battle of the Spurs, as visualised by the German artist Hans Burgkmair. The involvement of Imperial troops is greatly exaggerated, flags bearing the cross of Burgundy featuring prominently. English longbowmen are, however, clearly visible beneath one of these flags. (By courtesy of the Trustees of the British Museum)

No more than 40 Frenchmen were killed, but 120 notable prisoners were taken (including the Duc de Longueville, the Chevalier Bayard and, temporarily, La Palice himself). Meanwhile, the diversionary force had been driven off by the English light cavalry under Sir Rees Ap Thomas. The only practical gain from the encounter was the surrender, on 22 August, of the now demoralised garrison of Thérouanne.

Thérouanne was then destroyed on Henry's orders, freeing the entire English army to march east to the richer, but less well-defended city of Tournai. Once again we see the influence of the Holy Roman Emperor, for Tournai lay on the

The Battle of the Spurs: this version was painted some years after the event. In the centre of the picture a man is depicted in the improbable act of shooting a longbow from the back of a charging horse. Thérouanne is in the background. (Reproduced by gracious permission of HM the Queen)

borders of his own dominions. A heavy bombardment was soon followed by the city's capitulation, and Henry was able to make a triumphal entry on 25 September into this new English possession. Before this happy culmination of his first campaign took place, however, the king received news of a military feat which put his own in the shade.

Flodden Field

On his departure for France, Henry had taken the precaution of leaving the Earl of Surrey to defend England against possible Scottish incursions. The expected attack duly materialised. On the day that Henry accepted the surrender of Thérouanne,

James IV crossed into England with the largest and best equipped army ever to be assembled in Scotland.

Word soon reached the 70-year-old Earl of Surrey that the Scots were besieging Norham castle. He sent orders for the troops of the northern counties to muster at Newcastle, and marched thither himself with his own band of 500 men. Meanwhile the Scots took Norham, along with the lesser strongholds of Wark, Etal and Ford. On 3 September Surrey moved north to Alnwick, where he awaited late arrivals; the final addition to his forces being his son Thomas Howard, Admiral of England, with 1,000 seasoned soldiers from the fleet. Reasonable estimates for the size of the English army vary from 12,000 to 26,000 men, the lower figure being the more plausible.

The old Earl had been disgruntled at having to miss out on the invasion of France, and wasted no

crossed the Till. From this position they turned south and marched towards Branxton Hill, immediately to the north of the Scottish position. Finding the enemy to his rear, James IV moved his forces from Flodden Hill to Branxton Hill, thus denying this eminence to the advancing English.

By late afternoon the Admiral was crossing a small brook known as Pallin's Burn, near the foot of Branxton Hill. Seeing the Scots coming into battle order above him, he sent an urgent message to his father, who had advanced by a more southerly route, crossing the Till at a ford. As the two English forces were brought into line, the Scottish guns opened fire. Although James IV possessed a fine train of artillery, it appears to have found some difficulty in shooting downhill; nevertheless, it did cause some of Lord Dacre's border levies to flee in panic. At this point the Earl of Surrey, seeing the Scots arrayed in four huge blocks (plus one smaller unit), felt compelled to reorganise his own forces. The small 'wing' units were paired, so that the English also had four large units. James IV then initiated an advance in echelon down the sodden slopes of Branxton Hill, hoping perhaps to catch the English as they were forming up.

time in marching to meet the Scots. By 6 September the English army lay at Wooler. Looking up the valley of the River Till they could descry Flodden Edge, on top of whose steep slopes the Scots had taken up an impregnable position. The Scottish host—much reduced by desertion—still probably outnumbered the English and to assault such a position would have been an act of lunacy. Surrey, nevertheless, knew that some action had to be taken despite the foul weather and the fact that his army was acutely short of supplies. After consulting his captains, the Earl put a singularly decisive plan into operation. He marched north to Bar Moor and then divided his army into two large bodies, each supported by two smaller 'wings'. On the morning of 9 September the first of these divisions, under the Admiral, marched north-west to Twizel Bridge and

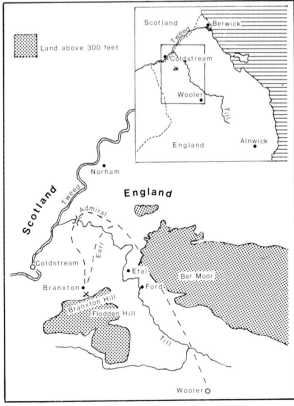

The Flodden campaign. Inset: the area in its geographical context.

7

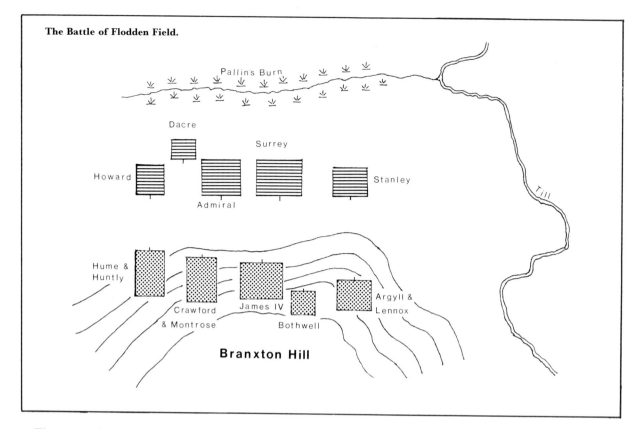

The Battle of Flodden Field.

First to make contact was the division under the Lords Hume and Huntly, who swept away most of the Lancashire and Cheshire men under Edmund Howard (a young nephew of the Earl of Surrey). Howard and his followers were able to fight their way to safety, however, and the situation was saved by a timely charge from Lord Dacre's remaining men. There is some dispute as to whether or not Dacre's Borderers were mounted when they charged: on balance, it seems most likely that they were not. Whatever the case, they managed to halt Hume and Huntly, and a 'stand-off' ensued. This was possibly because each side considered their duty to be done, but may also have been because both sides consisted largely of Borderers—notoriously reluctant to come to handstrokes, except in pursuit of their own local feuds.

Next into action was the Admiral's division, consisting of a large contingent sent by the Bishop of Durham and some northern gentry as well as the men from the fleet. They received the charge of the Earls of Crawford and Montrose. In contrast to events to their left, this Scottish division, disorganised by the steep and slippery hillside, met with a bloody repulse and both Earls were killed. The main Scottish division, under James IV himself, augmented by the smaller unit under the Earl of Bothwell, crashed into the Earl of Surrey's division, which consisted largely of Yorkshiremen. Here, too, the impact of the Scots was reduced by the terrain, and a ferocious hand-to-hand fight developed.

On the English left, Sir Edward Stanley with his Lancashire levies faced a body of Highlanders under the Earls of Lennox and Argyll. English archery had proved ineffective elsewhere along the line due to the heavy armour of the Scottish nobility and gentry who made up the front ranks of their pike-blocks. The more lightly armed Highlanders proved to be far more vulnerable. Removing their shoes and boots to improve their grip, Stanley's men climbed the slippery hill, and caught the Scots in the flank. A rout ensued, with the Highlanders scattering across the battlefield. Eventually the pursuing Lancashire men reached the scene of the

Flodden Field: another Burgkmair woodcut. James IV lies dead in the foreground, and the Scots begin to flee. Although the artist depicts the Scots in German-style costumes similar to many others in his battle scenes, the English are very distinctive, both in clothing and in armament. (British Library)

8

fight between James IV and Surrey. Here lay the king's corpse, within yards of his adversary, and around lay the dead and dying of the king's shattered division. Hume and Huntly could only withdraw, leaving the blood-soaked field to the English.

English losses had been surprisingly low, probably less than 1,000. The most moderate contemporary estimate of Scottish losses (from a Scot) is 5,000. The cataclysmic effect on Scotland was magnified by the disproportionate number of casualties suffered by the nobility, most of whom had followed their King's example and entered into the thick of the fray.

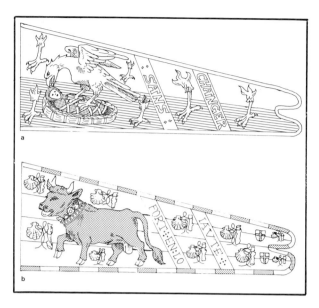

Standards borne at Flodden: *(a) Stanley.* **Upper half: tawny. Lower half: green. Eagle's legs, eagle and cradle: gold. Swaddling clothes: red, bound with gold.** *(b) Dacre.* **Ground: alternately yellow and blue, fringed white and red. Bull: red with golden crown and horns. Badges: white staffs and scallop shells entwined with red knots. Shields of St George in the fly. Both standards would have borne the cross of St George at the hoist.**

War with France, 1522–23

England's next involvement in a war came only after a lengthy period of diplomatic manoeuvring. At one point, after Henry VIII's celebrated meeting with Francis I of France at the 'Field of the Cloth of Gold', it seemed that England would become an ally of France. However, when Henry again went to war, it was as an ally of the Emperor Maximilian's successor, Charles V, and the rebel Constable of France, Charles of Bourbon.

A small force was sent to France in 1522 under the Earl of Surrey (Thomas Howard—the Admiral at Flodden). Apart from an abortive attempt to besiege Hesdin, Surrey's force did little except ravage the countryside, the main English effort being reserved for the following year.

During the summer of 1523 an army of some 9,000 men was shipped to Calais and placed under the command of the Duke of Suffolk. Meanwhile Surrey was sent north to the Scottish border, where the troops of the northern shires had been mobilised to face the threat of invasion. As a result of the fecklessness of the Scots' leader, the Duke of Albany, this was a threat which never materialised.

Suffolk was forced to wait at Calais until 20

September for the arrival of 3,500 German troops led by Floris, Count of Buren. The original plan had been to lay siege to Boulogne, but Buren and the other Imperial agents attached to the army pressed for a deeper thrust to be made into France. Eventually, despite the lateness of the season and Henry VIII's misgivings, their counsel prevailed. With France's main forces engaged in the south, Suffolk was able to make good headway. Striking for the middle Somme, he captured Bray after a gallant assault. Crossing the river the English army swept on to take Roye and, on 28 October, received the surrender of Montdidier after a bombardment. Paris itself was now only 50 miles distant; but fate turned against the English.

Severe weather set in, causing many casualties from exposure and frostbite. News arrived of the defeat of Bourbon in Provence. Most significantly, the army had become demoralised. The large Welsh contingent in Suffolk's force had already shown signs of indiscipline; it now went on strike, shouting 'Home, home!' The situation was exacerbated by the difficulty of transporting money beyond the Somme with which to pay the troops. With Paris seemingly within his grasp Henry VIII ordered Suffolk to hold on and await reinforcements; but, faced with large-scale desertion, Suffolk was forced to retreat, and finally to disband his army—ending one of the more pointless episodes of English military history.

For almost two decades following 1523 Henry VIII was forced to eschew all thought of military conquests, as he wrestled with the problems involved in repudiating his first wife, Catherine of Aragon, and eventually, breaking with the Church of Rome. The late 1530s in particular were a period of crisis. In 1537 resentment over Henry's religious policy led to a rebellion in the northern counties—the so-called 'Pilgrimage of Grace'. This revolt was suppressed without a battle taking place; the king was forced to rely upon negotiation and subterfuge as he was unable to raise sufficient forces rapidly enough to meet the rebels on equal terms.

In 1539 the threat of invasion loomed. It was widely rumoured that Charles V and Francis I—now at peace—were intending to mount a joint 'crusade' against the schismatic king of England. During the spring of that year the whole of England's military strength was mobilised to meet this threat; but Francis and Charles had other fish to fry, and by midsummer the danger had passed. Within three years the Emperor and the French king were once more at war with one another.

A Return to War

The renewal of the Hapsburg-Valois struggle allowed Henry, as a recent biographer has written, to 'resume what had once been for him the principal business of his reign and end his life as he had begun it, at war'. The first target of his aggression was Scotland—still a thorn in England's side. The defeat and capture of 500 English raiders at Haddon Rig, in August 1542, prompted Henry to attempt, once and for all, to impose his will upon the Scots. His demands that they should end their alliance with France, sign a perpetual peace with England and repatriate the Haddon Rig prisoners, were rejected by King James V. Consequently the Duke of Norfolk was sent with a substantial army to mount a punitive raid, but due to the failure of his supply arrangements Norfolk was forced to return to Berwick after only a week.

The Scottish response to this incursion resulted in an even greater débâcle. The 10–18,000-man army which James V despatched to invade Cumberland was riven by internal dissension, and a sudden attack by less than 4,000 English Borderers, under Sir Thomas Wharton, proved sufficient to precipitate a rout. Only 20 Scots were killed, but 1,200 were captured after having become bogged in waterlogged Solway Moss. They included two earls, five barons and 500 gentlemen; the English had lost just seven men. This humiliation proved too much for James V, who died shortly afterwards leaving his six-day-old daughter, Mary, as Queen of Scots.

Unfortunately, Henry VIII failed to seize this golden opportunity to resolve the Scottish problem. He did not take immediate and decisive military action, but instead used the noble prisoners taken at Solway Moss in an attempt to form a pro-English party in Scotland. The leader of this group, the Earl of Arran, proved to be no match politically for the pro-French Cardinal Beaton. By the time this fact became clear to Henry VIII it was too late to take military action, for to do so would have alienated all pro-English sentiment in Scotland. In any case, by 1543 Henry's attention had turned away from the

The victor of Flodden, Thomas Howard, Earl of Surrey, was created 2nd Duke of Norfolk in recognition of his feat. He was over 80 when he died, but this sepulchral brass shows him as a much younger man. His armour also pre-dates his death, the small tassets and full mail skirt being reminiscent of the previous century. We should not, of course, deduce from this that the duke could not afford up-to-date armour, but should note that the engraver, working in the 1520s, saw nothing incongruous in depicting this style. (By courtesy of the Trustees of the British Museum)

conflict in the north and was firmly focused on the war that was now raging in Europe.

The 'Enterprise of Boulogne'

An anti-French alliance between Henry VIII and Charles V was signed early in 1543. It came too late to allow for the organisation of a full-scale campaign for that year. Instead, a token force of 5,000 English troops under Sir John Wallop were despatched to the aid of the Emperor in the Low Countries. A joint attack on a massive scale was planned for 1544.

Charles Brandon, Duke of Suffolk, who played a major rôle in the continental expeditions of 1523 and 1544. He was Henry VIII's brother-in-law and, perhaps, his only close friend. (By courtesy of the Trustees of the British Museum)

Each monarch was to advance on Paris with over 40,000 men, Charles striking westward through Champagne, while Henry advanced south from Calais. It is doubtful whether Henry VIII ever accepted this 'Enterprise of Paris' as a serious proposition; even before his army set sail he appears to have narrowed his objective to the capture of towns and territory adjacent to the English 'Pale' around Calais.

Henry certainly fulfilled his obligations with regard to his army's size. The expeditionary force was the largest ever to have left these shores, totalling over 42,000 men, including numerous mercenaries and 4,000 auxiliaries sent by the Emperor. As in 1513, the vanguard and rearguard of the army preceded the main body, which was to be commanded by the king in person, with the assistance of the Duke of Suffolk. The vanguard, under the Duke of Norfolk (the Admiral at Flodden and Earl of Surrey during the war of 1522–23), and the rearguard under Lord Russell, landed during June.

It was not until the beginning of July, however, that they advanced, on Imperial advice, to Montreuil. This town had to be taken if the English army was to advance further into France. Unfortunately the English commanders set about their task in a distinctly half-hearted fashion, not even managing to fully surround the town. Norfolk, the senior of the pair, appears to have entirely lost the aggression which had previously characterised his generalship. The exasperated Russell was unable to stiffen the Duke's resolve, despite being 'very plain with him . . . . diverse times'.

In the meantime the main body of the army, numbering 16,000 men, had disembarked and, led by the Duke of Suffolk, had invested Boulogne on 19 July. The king, having tarried for ten days at Calais, rode out to supervise the siege of Boulogne on 26 July. Henry VIII was no longer the active young warrior of 1513, but his presence seems to have ensured that this siege was prosecuted with a good deal more vigour than that of Montreuil. A heavy bombardment was begun, coupled with attacks upon the out-works of the fortress.

The lightly fortified lower town and a Roman lighthouse—known as the 'Old Man' to the English—were soon captured. On 1 September the *fausse-braye* of the castle, which protected the upper-town, was captured after a courageous assault. The English failed to break into the castle itself, finding 'great resystance of men, Hayleshot, and Rampaires of Stone and earthe, so that they coulde not entre'. The incessant bombardment and the explosion of mines under the castle walls persuaded the French of the hopelessness of their position, however, and terms for the surrender of the 1,630 surviving members of the garrison were agreed on 13 September.

At Montreuil, serious siege work had hardly commenced. English troops had raided as far south as Abbeville, and Norfolk was keen to persuade the king that the garrison of Montreuil was in dire straits: 'glad to eat of a cat well larded and called it dainty meat'. The sad truth was that the besieging force was as much in danger of starvation as the besieged. French raids on the supply convoys sent from St Omer were a serious problem, and Norfolk's German horsemen made plain their chagrin at having to wear out their horses on escort duty. 'Strange and horrible' weather had brought sickness to the camp and destroyed vital forage.

This sorry state of affairs was brought to an

abrupt end by the news that on 18 September, the day of Henry VIII's triumphant entry into Boulogne, the Emperor, having spent most of the campaigning season besieging the frontier fortress of St Dizier, had signed a separate peace with Francis I. With the threat from the east thus removed the French were now in a position to send a large force against the English. Accordingly, Henry VIII authorised Norfolk and Russell to withdraw via St Omer, leaving for the safety of England himself on 30 September. Contrary to their orders, Norfolk and Russell retreated to Boulogne via Etaples, abandoning much of their baggage in the process. Close on their heels came the Dauphin with a large army, possibly as many as 30,000 men. At this juncture something approaching a state of panic appears to have prevailed among the English commanders, for on 3 October they made a precipitate withdrawal to Calais. To the king's immense fury only 4,000 men were left to defend his newly-won prize.

The 'Camisade of Boulogne'

The Dauphin duly appeared before the town on 7 October. His reconnaissance quickly revealed that the breaches made in the walls of the lower town by the English artillery had not yet been sealed; furthermore, the watch-keeping of the occupiers was extremely lax. Consequently, he resolved to launch a night attack, or 'camisade', on 9 October. With white shirts over their coats and armour as an aid to recognition (this was the feature that gave such operations the name 'camisade'), 23 companies of selected French and Italian infantry were to make the initial assault. Large bodies of Swiss and Landsknechts were held in reserve.

Initially success was achieved, as the French poured into the lower town driving all before them. However, their commander De Tais was forced to withdraw, wounded by an arrow. Other French captains also withdrew their men, due to a false alarm about the English having recaptured the breaches. At this point the French commanders in the town lost control of their men, who set about plundering the houses and the copious stores abandoned by the fleeing English.

Meanwhile, in the upper town the garrison was being rallied and re-formed. Under the command of Sir Thomas Poynings they charged back into the lower town, throwing their previously victorious foes into confusion. The French were driven out of the town as fast as they had entered, with the loss of 800 men killed or taken prisoner. The French reserves arrived too late to retrieve the situation.

After this débâcle, the French decided to postpone further attempts to recapture Boulogne until the next campaigning season. Marshal de Biez was left to keep watch on the town from the south side of the River Liane, the harbour and town being on the north shore of the estuary.

1545–1546

The year 1545 was one of crisis for Henry VIII. Deprived of the aid of Charles V, he was forced to face the might of France alone. A seaborne invasion of England was confidently expected, and the fate of

North-eastern France.

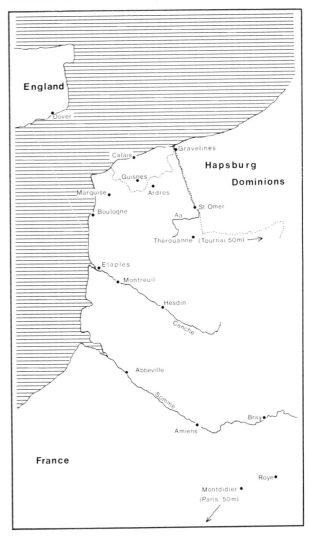

This French parade shield probably depicts the retreat of the English from Montdidier in 1523. Longbowmen are certainly visible in the ranks of one army. (By permission of the Trustees of the Wallace Collection)

Boulogne hung in the balance. Three separate forces were mustered in southern England to face the invasion threat: the Duke of Norfolk commanded in Essex, Suffolk was in charge in Kent and Lord Russell was commander in the west.

Luckily for the English, the French proved unable to press home their advantage. The potential invasion disintegrated into a series of inconclusive naval actions along the southern coast, the only notable incident being the accidental sinking of the *Mary Rose* during one of these engagements. French troops did make a small-scale landing near Bonchurch on the Isle of Wight, but this was easily repulsed.

Prior to launching his invasion of France in the previous year, Henry VIII had attempted to intimidate the Scots by sending the Earl of Hertford to Leith with a seaborne army. Leith, Edinburgh, and many smaller places were burnt as Hertford moved inland and then marched south towards Berwick, leaving a swathe of devastation in his wake. In February 1545, however, the Scots proved that they were still a force to be reckoned with, inflicting a sharp defeat on an English raiding force at Ancrum Moor. It was not until September that Henry was able to retaliate by sending Hertford on another destructive raid of the Lowlands, thus perpetuating this doleful conflict, which was to drag on into the reign of Edward VI.

In France, the war followed a similarly indecisive course during 1545. At Boulogne the French were unable to muster sufficient men to invest the town fully. The English garrison was always too weak to dislodge the French from their earthwork fortifications on the south bank of the river, despite several attempts. The French did achieve a measure of success, but this came in the county of Oye, to the east of Calais, where Marshal de Biez attacked with 20,000 men and forced the English back on Calais. The French soldier and commentator, Montluc, gives an interesting description of an attack on an English earthwork fort, in which he took part; otherwise few reliable details of this campaign survive.

In September 1545 Henry VIII appointed as Lieutenant of Boulogne the wayward soldier-poet Henry Howard, Earl of Surrey, he also appears to have pandered to the intense personal concern

This contemporary drawing depicts an English man-at-arms: possibly Henry VIII himself. (British Library)

which had led Henry VIII to pour vast sums of money into the defence of his conquest. Surrey's father, the Duke of Norfolk, did not share, along with others, the king's determination to hold on to Boulogne at all costs. At the end of September 1545 he wrote advising his son to 'animate not the King too much for the keeping of Boulogne; for who so doth at length shall get small thank'.

In January 1546 Surrey finally overreached himself. With 2,600 foot and all the horse of Boulogne, he attacked a French supply column which was escorted by 500 horse and 4,000 Landsknecht foot. The English cavalry, in a gallant charge, soon put their French counterparts to flight and began to destroy the enemy waggons. Unfortunately for Surrey, his infantry, mainly English but with some Italian arquebusiers attached, proved no match for the Landsknechts. Although the French convoy was virtually destroyed, the English lost 205 men, including 22 gentlemen; several standards were lost to the enemy.

Thomas Howard, 3rd Duke of Norfolk, played a central rôle in the military and political affairs of Henry VIII's reign. After proving his mettle at Flodden, he led forces against France in 1522 and Scotland in 1523, and finally commanded the vanguard during the 1544 expedition. (By courtesy of the Trustees of the British Museum)

This minor disaster led to the replacement of Surrey by Hertford, the rising star on the Tudor military and political scene. Apparently the king toyed with the idea of sending a 30,000-man army to France in 1546. In the event, Hertford's role was limited to manoeuvring for advantage during the period preceding the signing of a peace treaty between England and France at Camp on 7 June.

Thus the military history of Henry VIII's reign came to a close. The Treaty of Camp provided for the return of Boulogne to France, after a period of eight years, in return for an indemnity. As Tournai had also been restored to the French in 1519, England had no concrete gains to show for the ruinous expenditure involved in mounting the three invasions of France. Indeed, it might also be said that opportunities to bring the Scottish imbroglio to a successful conclusion were spurned, due to Henry VIII's senseless quest for glory overseas.

Recruitment and Organisation

Henry VIII's army was not, of course, a permanent force: the king had only minimal standing forces at his disposal. Chief among these were the Yeomen of the Guard—increased, during the opening years of Henry's reign, from 200 to 600 men. It is interesting to note that their rôle was not confined to that of royal bodyguard. In the spring of 1513 they were marched to Plymouth, in readiness for a proposed invasion of Brittany. In December 1544, long after the king's return to England, the garrison of Boulogne included 185 Yeomen of the Guard.

Henry could also count on the gentlemen of his household. In the first year of his reign he organised 50 young men of noble blood into a mounted bodyguard. Known as the 'King's Spears', they served as men-at-arms, each being supported by a lighter cavalryman, two mounted archers and a page. Expensive to maintain, this unit was dissolved within six years; in 1539 though, Henry created a similar force called the 'Gentleman Pensioners'. During 1544, 73 of these gentlemen accompanied their king to Boulogne. As individuals, they could also be assigned to other duties: in 1545 Sir George

One of a series of engravings made from contemporary murals at Cowdray House in Sussex (since destroyed). Here we see the departure of the middle ward of the English army from Calais in July 1544. (National Army Museum, London)

Carew (who had been present at the siege of Boulogne), was drowned while captaining the *Mary Rose*. The only other permanent units available to Henry VIII were the garrisons, or 'crews', at Berwick and in Calais, and the other strongholds of the English 'Pale'.

Other troops were raised only when war threatened. Two main methods of recruitment were employed in England. Firstly, certain nobles and gentlemen could be paid to raise and lead contingents for service with the king's army; to this end they were given immunity from the zealously enforced restrictions on the maintenance of retainers. (These laws, codified by Henry VII and perpetuated by his son, were designed to curb the power of the nobility by preventing the creation of 'private armies'.) Secondly, there existed large county militias composed of men liable for military service under ancient obligations dating back to Anglo-Saxon times. In 1544 the southern counties of England (along with Wales), could provide over 90,000 men mustered under this system. Troops raised by both methods served side by side and could also be used to supplement the 'crews' in Berwick and the 'Pale'.

For overseas expeditions logistical limitations prevented more than a tithe of England's potential military strength from being shipped to the Continent. In the resulting armies, contingents raised under contract tended to predominate. Conversely, when England was threatened with invasion, the militia was invariably mustered. The levies of the northern counties were earmarked for service against the Scots, while those of the south were to face the French. These were the men who formed the bulk of the army at Flodden Field and who stood-to in southern England during the invasion scares of 1539 and 1545.

Armies could be augmented by auxiliaries recruited outside this framework. In the French campaign of 1523, a band of English adventurers known as the 'Krekers', or 'Crackers', played a prominent rôle. They served for loot and appear to have been brave, if undisciplined. Similar troops were recruited in London in 1545, for service at Boulogne. For the invasion of France in 1544, 600 Irish warriors were enlisted. These 'Kern' made an impact which belied their small number, due to their success at skirmishing, raiding and cattle stealing. According to the Duke of Norfolk, the French thought them '*Gens mervelous sauvaige*'.

A further supplement was provided by the hiring of foreign mercenaries. Mercenary troops took part in all of Henry VIII's continental campaigns and also served on a smaller scale against the Scots.

These men were not enlisted merely to increase the size of English armies, but rather to make up for deficiencies in certain troop-types. England did not produce large numbers of pikemen, arquebusiers or heavy cavalry; consequently, these were the types most commonly hired.

Landsknecht pikemen were present in every force

The siege of Boulogne, as depicted at Cowdray House. At bottom left stands the king's camp. Henry himself appears at the far right, overseeing operations. At centre left a group of Irish auxiliaries can be discerned, driving cattle ahead of them. The artillery is being concentrated on one section of the walls, in the hope of creating a breach. (National Army Museum, London)

sent to the Continent, including the ill-fated expedition to Spain in 1511. Heavy cavalry were also hired from Germany, 'Burgundians' (from the Imperial provinces in the Low Countries) featuring in all three invasions of France. Artillerymen were also hired from the Low Countries, and paid according to the size of gun which they were to handle. In 1544–46 other mercenaries recruited included Spanish and Italian arquebusiers (who served in both France and Scotland) and 'Stradiots': Balkan light cavalry who had deserted from service with the French. In addition to true mercenaries, Landsknechts and men-at-arms were also 'borrowed' from the Emperor Charles V, with Henry VIII footing the wage bill. A contingent of this sort which attended Suffolk's army in 1523 was commanded by Floris von Isselstein, Count of Buren. His son, Maximilian, fulfilled the same rôle in 1544.

Of the relative merits and performances of these widely differing elements of Henry VIII's army, little direct evidence exists. Occasionally certain

Another engraving from Cowdray House depicts the camp of Henry VIII's ward at Marquise in 1544. The camp is shown suffering from the effects of the violent storm which occurred on the night of 25 July. (National Army Museum, London)

groups (such as the Welsh in 1523, or the Germans in 1544) are singled out for criticism; none, however, behaved badly enough to be excluded from later campaigns. (Welsh contingents served again in 1544, and German mercenaries played an important rôle in the warfare in France during 1545–46.)

Taking a wider view, it might be said that the lack of discipline and the low morale apparent in some English armies of this period were largely due to their heterogenous composition. Retinues and militia contingents were not bound to their leaders by strong 'feudal' loyalties, and indiscipline stemming from elements such as the Welsh, Landsknechts or 'Crackers' could be infectious. Although staunch in the defence of their homeland, English armies seem to have required the presence of the king himself to motivate them while overseas; only he could provide the authority, prestige and focus for loyalty needed to hold the disparate elements of his army together.

The organisation of Henry VIII's army was based on companies of 100 men. This is abundantly apparent from surviving documents. Contingents brought by nobles or gentlemen, or provided by towns or parishes, could be of almost any size from two to 2,000 men. While in the field, however, smaller groups were brigaded together while the larger ones were provided with numerous captains. Naturally, company strengths could fluctuate due to the exigencies of campaigning; nevertheless, 100 men, led by a captain and a 'petty' captain (at half the captain's rate of pay), was the norm.

At a higher level, armies were generally divided into three huge 'wards', along medieval lines: namely, the Vanguard, Battle and Rearguard. This unwieldy system was intended more for administrative convenience than for battlefield use. At Flodden, Surrey, with his relatively small army, adopted a formation which comprised two main bodies, each supported by two 'wings': a deployment which proved flexible enough to resolve itself into four large bodies before battle was joined. In the same year, when Henry VIII marched out of Calais with the Battle of his invasion army, he too deployed 'wings' to support the main body of his 'ward'. In 1544 the three 'wards' were so large (13,000, 16,000 and 13,000 men respectively) as to be able to operate as two separate armies.

The most remarkable feature of this organisational structure was the lack of any intermediate unit between the 100-man company and the 'ward' of thousands. The Spanish had developed the *colunela* (1,000–1,500 men) in the first decade of the century and, by the mid-1530s, had begun to establish the famous *tercio* (3,000 men). In 1531 Francis I of France created his infantry 'Legions' (6,000 men). Even the Landsknechts habitually organised themselves into companies of 400. England, however, remained oblivious to these developments: only *ad hoc* groupings of companies under a single commander provided tactical units of a useful size. This was as true in 1544 as it had been in 1513. Thus Henry VIII's army stood outside the mainstream of European military organisation, apart from reflecting the general rise in overall army size which was a feature of the period.

The siege of Boulogne, as depicted at Cowdray House. The lower town and the harbour, already in English hands, are to the right. At far right is the Roman lighthouse known as the 'Old Man'. Artillery is massed in the foreground, including two huge wooden 'cannons' with small guns strapped to them—these were apparently constructed to over-awe the garrison of Boulogne. One at least seems to have survived in the Tower of London until 1841. (National Army Museum, London)

Supply and other auxiliary services were generally even less systematically organised than the fighting troops. A mass of non-combatants would accompany every army: pioneers and labourers, millers and bakers, cartwrights and butchers, even Cornish miners for siege operations. (In 1544–46 female camp-followers also appeared, although in lesser numbers than with most European armies.) Supplies were purchased from individual merchants by royal commissioners. Prices were fixed by decree; unfortunately this did not guarantee the quality of the goods. In 1545, for instance, the garrison of Boulogne were dismayed to receive many barrels of meal and beef which had been rendered inedible due to careless packing.

Distribution was a still greater problem. Each army was provided with a quota of waggons and waggoners; detailed regulations concerning their conduct were laid down in the aftermath of the 1523 campaign. However, to convey supplies to the army from their source (supply dumps known as 'staples'), further transport was necessary. It was the difficulty of providing this that contributed to the abrupt end of the campaign in France in 1523 and that of Norfolk in Scotland, 19 years later. Furthermore, it was lack of supply which precipitated the battle of Flodden Field *and* prevented the exploitation of the resulting victory.

The most common complaint from commanders in the field, regarding supply, was of a shortage of beer. Apparently no English army could remain long in the field without it. In 1544 Norfolk wrote from outside Montreuil that his men had drunk no beer for ten days: 'which is strange for English men to do with so little grudging'. The importance of giving the troops what they were accustomed to is emphasised by the sad decline of the force sent to Spain in 1511 who: 'did eate of the Garlicke with all

This map of Boulogne was made by John Rogers, the engineer in charge of fortifying the town after its capture. At bottom left is the Roman *pharos* (the 'Old Man') surrounded by newly raised ramparts. Above this is Boulogne itself; the lower town extends down to the harbour from the more heavily fortified upper town. The lines of fortification south of the river indicate where the French were encamped during 1545–46. (British Library)

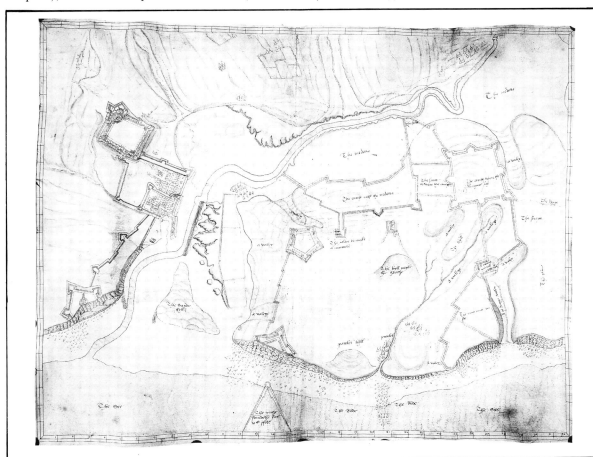

meates, and drank hote wynes in the hote weather, and did eate all the hote frutes that thei could gette, which caused their bloudde so to boyle in their bellies, that there fell sicke three thousand of the flixe [dysentery] and thereof died XVIII hundred men'. Thus chronicler Edward Hall gives us an early example of the failure of the Englishman abroad to come to terms with the local cuisine!

For each expedition to France, supplies and the waggons to transport them, were secured (with Imperial aid) from the Low Countries. However, as the armies moved away from their bases their lines of supply became more difficult to maintain, and increasingly vulnerable to attack. During the late summer of 1544 it became so difficult to safely supply the force at Montreuil from St Omer that it was proposed to move the 'staple' from there to Gravelines, and to send the supplies via Calais and Boulogne. Ambushing of waggon convoys became a salient feature of the French campaigns; this is especially noticeable in the desultory warfare of 1545–46.

Equipment

Infantry

In the field of military technology, the first half of the 16th century was a period of rapid change in western Europe; however, to a large extent Henry VIII's England stood aloof from continental developments. The most obvious manifestation of this insularity was in the continued reliance upon the traditional bill and bow as the main offensive weapons. The reputation gained by the longbow during the Hundred Years' War had not yet been seriously challenged: most Englishmen still regarded it as the supreme arbiter of battle. The king himself took pride in his ability as an archer, and issued proclamations encouraging the practice of archery. The demand for bow-staves was immense, many being imported; those of wood grown in the warm Mediterranean climate were especially favoured. Merchants were required to bring a quota of bow-staves into the country with each cargo of imported goods.

It would seem that the equipment of an archer of this period differed little from that of his predecessors who had fought at Agincourt. In 1531 an Italian observer was able to describe them as fighting 'in the old fashion, with bow, sword, buckler, sallet, and a two-pronged iron stake to resist a charge from the enemy's horse'. Archers' stakes are regularly mentioned in contemporary documents; they generally appear to have been made of wood, shod or 'garnished' with iron. One difference between the Tudor archer and his 15th-century counterpart was the former's use of a quiver. While these seem previously to have been a rarity, clear references to them exist from Henry VIII's reign. In 1513 the Earl of Northumberland equipped his archers with quivers in his livery colours (see Plate B3). A royal proclamation of 1542 sets the price of various items of military equipment, including 'leather cases' for arrows. In both cases the quiver appears to have been suspended from the waist by a 'girdle'.

Although no contemporary quivers have survived, several bracers, worn by archers on the inside of their left arm, have been preserved. Apart from the example in the British Museum a number of bracers were recovered from the wreck of the *Mary Rose*, made of either leather or horn. Interestingly, no 'tabs' (for protecting the fingers of the right hand while drawing and releasing the bowstring) were found on the *Mary Rose*. Dr Margaret Rule points out that, as it is unlikely that none survived, it might be concluded that the calloused fingers of experienced archers did not require such protection.

Despite its continued popularity, the English bow was not destined to win any more great victories. Indeed, at Flodden Field, the most important battle of Henry VIII's reign, the issue was decided by the bow's 'companion' weapon, the bill. The English bill, often called a 'brown' or 'black' bill due to a coating of rust or varnish, was a crude but effective weapon, much closer to its origins as an agricultural implement than its continental counterpart (see Plate A). Naturally it was an easier weapon to master than the bow, and did not require constant practice. Consequently billmen considerably outnumbered bowmen in every English army of the period. This disparity is particularly evident in the muster lists of 1539 and 1544. The situation at Flodden was, of course, tailor-made for the English billmen. The Scots were inexperienced in handling pikes, and the slippery slope which disordered their advance gave the handier bill a great advantage.

The failure of pike against bill at Flodden did not discredit the pike as a weapon. Henry VIII was shrewd enough to realise that an army solely armed with bill and bow could not hope to face the French on equal terms. English troops were seldom equipped with what they called 'Morris' (Moorish) pikes. At a muster of the London Trained Bands in 1539, the pikemen were thought particularly impressive; probably due to their relative novelty. Even in 1544 the retinues of the gentlemen of the Privy Chamber could only muster 380 pikemen, compared with 1,073 billmen. To increase his army's pike strength, Henry VIII had to look abroad: Landsknecht pikemen were hired for every continental expedition.

Mercenaries also had to be recruited to make good the lack of arquebusiers in England. This was evident during the war of 1544–46: Henry VIII and his commanders were well aware of the important rôle being played by firearm infantry in contemporary warfare. In 1544 a royal proclamation was issued encouraging the use of arquebuses. However, with the coming of peace in 1546, this was quickly cancelled by another proclamation banning the use of such weapons. It seems that the king was not keen to see the population at large arming itself with guns, preferring to hire foreign specialists over whom he had more control. With plenty of experienced archers still available, and considering the relative cost-effectiveness of bows, there was little to induce Henry to re-equip his army with firearms. Arquebuses were imported, but not on a very lavish scale. It is indicative of the limited rôle envisaged for the arquebus that in 1544 the king's agent in Antwerp was seeking to buy wheellock weapons, as opposed to the more normal (and cheaper) match-locks, regarding the latter as 'very slender gear not meet to be sent to His Majesty'.

One other infantry weapon sometimes men-

This contemporary drawing shows an English army on the march. (British Library)

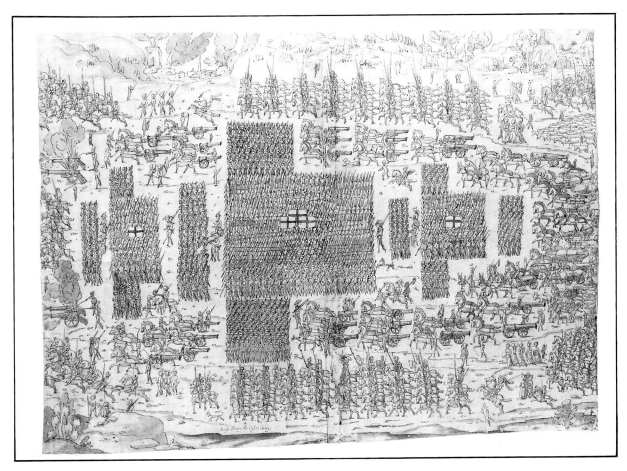

tioned is worthy of note: that most basic of weapons, the simple spear, was still in use in Henry VIII's army. Specifically described, in at least one document, as 'long', the spear was particularly favoured by the Welsh. The muster list for Denbighshire in 1539 shows more spearmen than billmen. Unfortunately there seems to be no reference to this rather anachronistic weapon's use in battle.

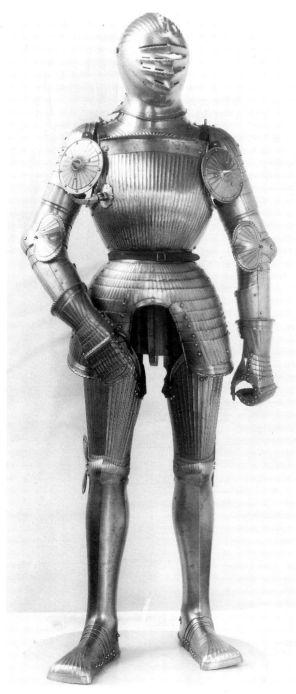

Cavalry

Cavalry made up only a small proportion of English armies at this period. The great victory of Flodden was won by infantry alone; and 31 years later the army for the invasion of France had less than 4,000 cavalry, compared with over 28,000 infantry. In the same year the levies of the northern shires, mustered for war with the Scots, could show 2,500 cavalry, as against 14,000 foot. The proportion of 'true' cavalry was even lower than these figures suggest, as mounted archers (who dismounted to fight) were always included in the lists of 'horse'.

The greatest deficiency was in heavy cavalry. The renaissance of the man-at-arms as a battlefield force, which had been spearheaded by the creation of the French *Compagnies d'Ordonnance*, had passed England by. The tradition of fighting dismounted lingered long among the English aristocracy. Moreover, suitable horses were not readily available in England. As late as 1557 an Italian commentator could write: 'With regard to heavy horse, good for men-at-arms, the island does not produce any, except a few in Wales . . . so the country cannot have any considerable quantity of heavy horse'. Most English 'heavy' cavalry were of the type known as demilances, wearing three-quarter armour and carrying the light lance that gave them their name.

Henry VIII was forced to supplement his cavalry by recruiting mercenaries or auxiliaries from the Holy Roman Empire. Despite the money he lavished on the hiring of such troops, he was generally disappointed by their quality. At the Battle of the Spurs the 'Burgundians' were careful not to charge until they saw that the French were beaten. Many of those hired in 1544 turned out to be *Reiter* ('Swarte Rutters' to the English), armed with 'boresperes and shorthandgonnes' (pistols). The men-at-arms, moreover, were not equipped with horse armour, which the English still thought important. The Germans explained that although they had previously used bards, they 'would never more adventure their lives with so cumbrous a thing'.

This suit of armour, made circa 1515–25, is a fine example of the fluted style popular in Germany during the first half of the 16th century. Many of the 'Burgundian' men-at-arms attached to Henry VIII's armies would have sported similar suits. (By permission of the Trustees of the Wallace Collection)

Flodden Field, 1513:
1: Billman
2: Archer, Sir Edward Stanley's contingent
3: Soldier, Earl of Surrey's contingent

A

France, 1513:
1: Halberdier, Earl of Northumberland's guard
2: Archer, Earl of Northumberland's contingent
3: Captain, Earl of Northumberland's contingent

Angus McBride

B

1: Border Horseman
2, 3: German Landsknechts

Angus McBride

C

1: Yeoman of the Guard, c. 1520
2: Yeoman of the Guard, c. 1538

2

1

Angus McBride

D

1: Man-at-arms, c. 1540
2: Halberdier, London Trained Bands, 1539

1

2

Angus McBride

E

France, 1544:
1: Pikeman, Vanguard
2: Demilance
3: Soldier, Thomas Caverden's contingent

Angus McBride

F

France, 1544:
1: Petty-captain of Foot
2: Landsknecht captain
3: Irish auxiliary

2

1

3

Angus McBride

G

France, 1544:
1: German cavalryman
2: Arquebusier

H

Light cavalry were more of an English speciality. They are referred to by several different names in contemporary documents, for example: 'Light Staves', 'Chasing Staves', 'Javelins' or 'Javelins with Targets'. The latter appear to have been equipped in a similar manner to the famous stradiots. A Venetian writing in 1551 describes some of the English light cavalry as 'armed in the Albanian fashion'. The cream of the English light horse were undoubtedly those recruited from the Northern Marches. They seem to have performed best when sent with expeditions to the Continent, away from the internecine feuding of border warfare. A contingent which accompanied Wallop's force in 1543 were said to have impressed Charles V himself. They were armed with 'northern staves': these appear to have been true light cavalry lances (as opposed to spears). William Damesell, seeking to purchase wood with which to make them in 1545, can only find wood for men-at-arm's 'staffs' in Antwerp; this he ignores as being too short and too dear.

One further type of light cavalryman was beginning to make an appearance by 1544: namely, the mounted arquebusier. A few of these 'demi-hakes on horseback' marched with the Battle of the expeditionary force—although apparently not enough. An Italian observer was quick to advocate their recruitment, in order to provide suitable escorts for supply convoys, a purpose for which the English were currently having to employ 'Almayne ruters, which with their great and heavy horses are scantly good but in a set battle'.

Armour

When it came to equipping his troops with armour, Henry VIII had once more to rely upon what could be procured from the Continent. England had no indigenous armour manufacturing industry of any importance. Henry attempted to remedy this by bringing over German armourers to work at his new armoury at Greenwich. Their output was so small, however, that the use of 'Greenwich' armour was limited to the king and his immediate circle. Accordingly, those who could afford it bought their harness from Italy, Germany and the Low Countries. The King himself sought to purchase no fewer than 100 Flemish armours for the gentlemen of his household in 1510. For those whose purses could not stretch to new imported armour, the alternative was to continue wearing suits which had gone out of fashion. The strongest evidence for this practice comes from contemporary church brasses (see page 38).

This bracer, for an archer's left wrist, is made from cuir-boulli (boiled leather). It is embossed with a crowned Tudor rose and the words 'IHS [Jesus] Helpe'. This inscription fits well with an Italian diplomat's comment on the army of 1513: 'There were few who failed daily to recite the office and our Lady's Rosary'. (By courtesy of the Trustees of the British Museum)

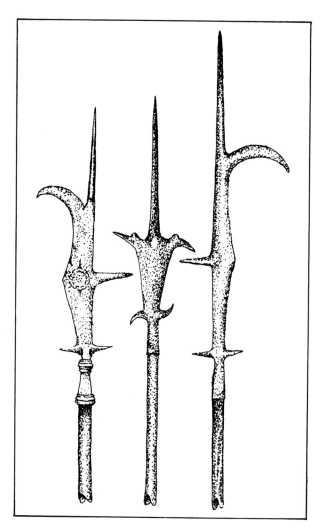

16th-century bills, showing a variety of shapes.

care taken in detailing these component parts suggests that the term 'Almain rivet' was loose enough to cover armour which lacked one or more of them.

Almain rivet appears generally to have been of low quality—the breast of the example preserved in Winchester (see Plate B1) is entirely worn through in one place—and this is certainly reflected in the cost of such armour. A royal proclamation of 1542 sets the price of the best quality Almain rivet at 7s 6d, whereas a suit of demilance armour costs 45s—six times as much.

Henry VIII purchased Almain rivet on a vast scale for issue to his troops. Warrants for payment exist for over 10,000 'pairs' of Almain rivet imported during 1512–13. An account of 1513 notes that 13,719 complete harnesses for footmen had been issued from the king's armoury during that year. In addition, Almain rivet was purchased by the nobility to equip their own retinues: the Earl of Northumberland provided his entire 500-man contingent (most of them archers) with such harness; and ten years later an inventory of the goods of Lady Hungerford (executed for murder) notes the presence of 120 'pairs' of Almain rivet.

If it is assumed that the lion's share of the 13,719 'pairs' issued from the Tower went to the army for France, and additional 'pairs' provided by men like the Earl of Northumberland are taken into account, it would seem likely that as many as half of the 20–30,000 infantry on that expedition were equipped with plate armour. For the great muster of the London Trained Bands in 1539 we are told that the Aldermen of the city were able to 'put a syde all soche as hadde jackes, coates of plate, coates of mayle and briganders, and appoynted none but soche as had whyte harness'. The prosperous Londoners were probably better equipped than the English militia forces as a whole. In the county muster lists for 1544, approximately a quarter of the troops are listed as 'with harness'. The proportion was undoubtedly higher in the army taken to France that year. The Duke of Norfolk's 'ward', for instance, were equipped with fustian or canvas 'arming doublets', indicating that it was intended to issue them with plate armour.

The quality of infantry armour does not seem to have improved; wear and tear took a heavy toll. In October 1544, during the celebrated 'Camisade' of

Henry VIII's reign coincided with a growing use of armour by the humble infantryman. In this area, at least, England did not lag behind the rest of Europe. Canvas jacks lined with metal plates, mail shirts, brigandines and jazerans (both made with many small, separate plates covered with cloth or leather), had long been used. Where Henry VIII's army really reflected continental developments was in the widespread use of specialised infantry plate armour. This type of harness is most commonly referred to in English sources as 'Almain [i.e. German] rivet'. This comprised a breast and back plate, usually complete with tassets; 'splints' for the arms; and a gorget. All these elements are specifically listed in a 1512 indenture to an Italian merchant; they are also mentioned in the list of the 'Equipage of the Earl of Northumberlend'. The

Boulogne, the French commentator Montluc noted 30 casks of 'German corselets' in the lower town. By July 1545, however, the commanders at Boulogne were complaining that out of 650 'pairs' of harness in the town only 200 were serviceable, of which 'the chief part rested on the captains and the petty captains in the fore ranks of battle, being armed with corselets'—a mere 200 men out of 5,000 foot present.

Ordnance

In the field of ordnance Henry VIII also relied heavily upon foreign imports. This is not to say that there were no guns made in England; indeed, Cornwall supplied the finest tin for use in the founding of brass guns. Nevertheless, English gunfounders could not match the expertise of their Flemish counterparts; thus it was to the Low Countries, and to men like Hans Poppenruyter of Malines, that Henry VIII turned for the manufacture of his best guns. Poppenruyter made numerous guns for Henry, including the famous 'Twelve Apostles' which were taken to France in 1513. Henry imported foreign talent as well as foreign guns: gunfounders were brought over from the Continent to work in the foundries at the Tower and at Houndsditch. A powerful train of artillery had already been accumulated by 1513: each 'ward' of the army was equipped with 60 guns, and with an additional 40 'organ' guns for anti-personnel use. The heavy artillery performed competently at Thérouanne and Tournai, but lack of a pitched battle restricted the usefulness of the 'organs'. The artillery was again limited to siege work in 1523 and 1544. Boulogne was bombarded by 95 guns and 50 mortars in 1544.

Guns were not the only ordnance used by Henry VIII's army. A drawing preserved in the British Library (from Cotton Ms Augustus III.a.) shows an English army employing various 'war-carts' or protected waggons (see page 42). Such vehicles are mentioned in contemporary documents as 'privy waggons' or 'close carts'. At the siege of Boulogne 20 of the former were present. An account submitted in 1544 by John Rogers, Henry VIII's chief military engineer, relates to the transportation of similar equipment: it mentions binding down the 'swordes of the engynes' and devices called 'shrympes'. A list of ordnance present at the siege of Boulogne mentions 50 of these 'shrimps'. They have been identified with some curious-looking machines depicted in murals of the 1544 campaign which once adorned the walls of Cowdray House in Sussex (see page 4). Once again, the absence of a major battle deprives us of any record of their use.

Other equipment used included caltrops and *chevaux de frise*: several surviving documents refer to 'latice galtrupps' and 'latice stakes', which were apparently made of iron. Their main use seems to have been the defence of military camps. Chronicler Edward Hall asserts that the camp at Thérouanne was defended by 'tryde harrowes' and 'spien trestyls'. Such devices may also have represented an attempt to compensate for the English army's lack of pikes. They are certainly symptomatic of the English attachment to the static mode of fighting, employed so successfully in France by their forebears.

From John Skelton's *Ballade of the Scottyshe Kynge*, **this print shows cavalry of the Flodden period. The knight wears outmoded 'gothic' armour. The light horseman wears a brigandine with short mail sleeves, but has full leg armour. (British Library)**

Uniforms

Henry VIII's reign is a period of fundamental importance for the study of the history of military costume. It witnessed a great change in conceptions of what sort of allegiances soldiers should be advertising in their garb, and saw the first tentative steps towards a national system of uniform.

At the outset of the reign the white coat was already firmly associated with the English soldier, so much so that the words 'white-coat' were almost interchangeable with the word 'soldier' in contemporary English. These coats were commonly emblazoned with the traditional English field sign: the red cross of St George. Even foreign troops in English service could be turned out in white. The 500 Landsknechts who, under the command of the Flemish captain Guyot, had accompanied the force sent to Spain in 1511 'were dressed', as Hall relates, 'all in white, whiche was cut so small that it could scarce hold together'. Evidently their eagerness to display English colours did not prevent them from maintaining their outlandish style of dress.

The accession of Henry VII to the throne in 1485

The armour of the common soldier. This jack probably post-dates Henry VIII's reign, but gives a good idea of their construction. The metal plates which provided the protection were held in place by the cord, clearly visible here, stitched through the canvas exterior. (By courtesy of the Trustees of the British Museum)

had added a new element to the traditional English colours. Green could now be added to the white to give a coat of the Tudor family livery colours. For the first half of Henry VIII's reign green and white coats are the type most frequently mentioned. The main reason for their widespread adoption was that the crown was responsible for paying for the coats of militia contingents: it was only natural that this 'coat money' should be used to provide coats in the king's colours.

Some units raised under contract were also clad in the royal livery. Surrey's retinue at Flodden Field was one such (see Plate A3); the Earl of

An early fruit of the foreign talent imported by Henry VIII to staff his armoury at Greenwich, this suit of armour was made for the king circa 1514–16. It boasts unusual metal 'bases' (in imitation of the cloth bases, often worn at this period). The horse bard is a Flemish-made import. (By courtesy of the Board of Trustees of the Royal Armouries)

Northumberland's contingent, taken to France in the same year, was another (see Plate B). A detailed list of the clothing provided by Northumberland has survived. Curiously, he combined the Tudor green and white of his men's coats with his own red and black livery colours, which appeared on their hats, quivers and flag-staffs. To add to this cocktail of colour, his men's coats bore not only the cross of St George, but also a Tudor (or perhaps Lancastrian) rose, and the crescent badge of his own family: the Percys. The actual uniform items were limited, as usual in this period, to a coat and bonnet. It is interesting to note that both Surrey and Northumberland came from families which had much to gain by the display of loyalty to the ruling dynasty, which the use of these colours represented.

Other units were provided with coats of a wide variety of colours, bearing an equally wide variety of cognisances. In 1511 the force sent to aid Margaret of Savoy in the Low Countries returned to England newly equipped by her in coats of red, yellow, green and white. The yellow and red probably represent Margaret of Savoy's livery colours. At Flodden Field, the contingent provided by the Stanley family (see Plate A2) wore coats emblazoned with the badges of the Stanleys and of the Bishopric of Ely (the bishop was a Stanley). An early poem describes them thus:

'Every bearne [man] had on his breast
    brodered full fayre
A foot of the fayrest fowle that ever flew
    on winge,
With three crowns full cleare all of pure
    gold.'

A document of 1522 gives evidence of the king empowering the Earl of Shrewsbury to furnish the men of Shropshire and certain northern counties with liveries, badges and tokens; whether the livery in question was the king's or the red and black of the Earl is not revealed. The badges certainly sound as if they would have been the latter's: a silver talbot (hound).

The practice of small units being clad in their leader's colours certainly survived late into the reign. Peter Carew was captain of a company of 100 men in Wallop's 1543 expeditionary force; 'these', according to Carew's biographer, 'he clothed and apparelled at his own charges all in black, and they were named the Black Band'. The Carew arms were: Or, three lions passant in pale, sable.

A much larger force was the London Trained Bands. Their uniforms, as of 1539, are described in Hall's chronicle and in other sources. All, with the exception of officers and officials, were clothed in white, including their hose. Some had coats slashed to reveal red linings (see Plate E2). The 'meaner sorte of people' wore white cotton coats 'very curiously trimmed' with the arms of the city on front and back.

As the reign progressed, however, such individuality was increasingly suppressed in favour of uniform colours and field-signs dictated from above. In 1523 regulations governing what might be called the auxiliary services of the army stipulated that labourers should all wear a badge of a spade or mattock; carters were to have a badge of a horse-comb or a red cross. By 1544 clothing

This Norfolk church brass commemorates Sir Robert Clere, who died in 1529; his armour, however, is characteristic of an earlier date. He wears a breastplate with a separate plackart, a mail collar or standard instead of a gorget and one-piece tassets. (By courtesy of the Trustees of the British Museum)

regulations had become far more comprehensive. For the expedition to France the Battle and the Rearguard were provided with coats of red, guarded yellow; the Vanguard wore blue, guarded red. Details of the Vanguard's coat were sent to the Count of Buren, in order that he might clothe his own men correctly: 'The colours of the ward where Mons de Bure shall serve are blue and red, the body of the garment blue and a broad guard of III fingers broad red and one of the sleeves'. Most of the figures depicted in the engravings taken from the Cowdray House paintings appear to be wearing uniform coats. In the picture showing the departure of the king's ward from Calais, cavalry as well as infantry are clothed in them.

In a set of regulations concerning the clothing of the Vanguard it is stated that hose will also be provided 'the right hose to be all red and the lefte to be blew, with one stripe of three fingers brode of red upon the outside of his legg from the stock downwards'. The soldier was also to be issued with a cap 'to put his sculle or sallete in'. The same regulations place heavy restrictions upon the use of badges: 'noe gentleman nor other wear any manner of silke upon the garde of his coate, save only upon his left sleeve, and that no yeoman wear any manner of silke upon his saide coate; nor noe gentleman, nor yeoman to wear *any manner of badge*'. A red cross was to be sewn to the uppermost garment.

The issue of uniform on such a large scale must be considered a significant milestone in the development of English military costume. Moreover, it is probably more than coincidence that the blue, red and yellow colours reflect the tinctures of the royal arms. This contrasts with the purely dynastic connotations of the earlier green and white. This change of emphasis was also evident in the coats of the Yeomen of the Guard, which were changed from green and white to red in the middle of Henry VIII's reign (see Plate D). Nevertheless, it was to be many years before English troops were issued with a universally accepted national uniform. Evidence exists of contingents dressed in the livery colours of their commanders, and bearing their badges, only a few short years after Henry VIII's death. The tradition of the white coat also endured. In 1545 Lord Russell wrote that the men of Dorset, Somerset, Devon and Cornwall, whom he had mustered to face the threatened invasion, had provided themselves with white coats at their own expense. Contemporaries were still referring to soldiers as 'white-coats'.

Flags

A study of the flags borne by Henry VIII's army also reveals a movement toward national rather than personal insignia. In the early years of Henry's reign his armies marched under a similar mixture of flags to those which had fluttered over the heads of their medieval forebears. Pride of place was held by patriotic or religiously inspired standards and banners. (A banner is square, as opposed to the tapering or swallow-tailed shape of a· standard.) Flags made for the ill-fated Guienne expedition of 1511 included a standard displaying the cross of St George, surrounded by a green and white fringe, a green banner with a picture of St George and, rather optimistically, a banner bearing the arms of the Duchy of Guienne: gules, a lion passant-

This shield, fitted with a breech-loading matchlock pistol, was one of 40 made to order in the 1540s for issue to the king's bodyguard—presumably those members of the Yeomen of the Guard in closest attendance upon him. (By courtesy of the Board of Trustees of the Royal Armouries)

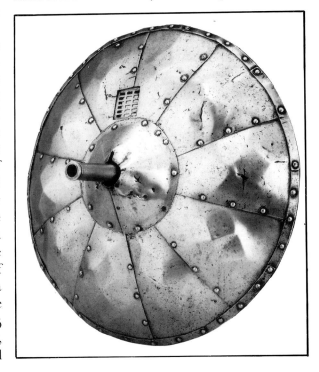

A product of Henry VIII's passion for innovation in the field of ordnance: this triple-barrelled, breech-loading cannon was made circa 1533 by Peter Baude, a French gunfounder working at Houndsditch in London. (By courtesy of the Board of Trustees of the Royal Armouries)

guardant, or. Hall mentions two religious flags which were carried by the king's ward during the 1513 invasion of France: one depicting the Virgin Mary and the other, which flew over the king's household servants, the Trinity. A banner bearing the arms of England flew over the king himself.

The chronicler notes that Henry also had with him his own personal standard: the Red Dragon (see page 46). It is evident, however, that this standard was not only flown in the king's presence: a red dragon standard was sent to the Earl of Surrey for use in the North in August 1512. The king's was certainly not the only personal standard to be seen in English armies of this period. A list of the standards carried by the captains of the army in France in 1513 survives in the British Library (Cotton Ms Cleopatra. C. V. f59.).

At Flodden Field, Surrey appropriated the ancient banner of St Cuthbert from Durham cathedral for use as the army's main flag; but the individual contingents which made up that army appear to have marched under the standards of their leaders. The author of the *Scottish Ffeilde*, an early ballad describing the battle, has James IV calling upon his herald to identify the various contingents by their standards. These include that of the Stanleys (see page 10), of which the herald is made to cry (somewhat melodramatically):

'Loe how he batters and beates the bird
    with his wings;
We are feared of yonder fowle, so fiercely
    he fareth.'

For the expedition of 1523 John Browne, the king's painter, made two banners bearing the Duke of Suffolk's arms. At the same time, however, Hall relates that the Duke himself issued the so-called 'Crackers' with a 'penon of St George': as an *ad hoc* unit they obviously lacked a standard of their own. The fact that the duke found it necessary to present them with one is indicative of the importance attached to such unit flags; not only did they identify the unit, but also played a vital rôle as a rallying point.

The Tudor livery colours were present on various flags from the outset of the reign. In 1512 waggons for the expeditionary force were to be provided with 'pencelles (small pennons) wrought upon buckram, white and green, and upon them a red rose with a crown imperial inoyled'. Interestingly, pennons of precisely this description are shown flying from small boats in the painting, now at Hampton Court, of the embarkation of Henry VIII at Dover prior to the 'Field of the Cloth of Gold'. By the end of Henry's reign flags bearing the cross of St George, often combined with the Tudor colours, appear to have predominated.

The engraving of the siege of Boulogne, taken from the Cowdray paintings, shows numerous flags (see page 19). In the foreground, near the king and some men-at-arms who may represent the Gentlemen Pensioners, a banner depicting St George and the Dragon and a standard bearing a crowned lion of England surrounded by *fleurs-de-lys* can clearly be seen. Less distinctly, in the distance, a horseman can be seen carrying the standard of Sir Anthony Browne, Master of the King's Horse. This latter may be ignored, however, being the artist's flattering reference to the man who commissioned his work: Sir Anthony Browne himself.

All the other flags bear the cross of St George, some combining it with stripes or bars which are known to have been white and green in the original painting. Flags with crosses and bars of this sort are also in evidence in some of the contemporary drawings of English armies in the British Library manuscript: Augustus III.a.; unfortunately, the ink-and-wash style in which they are executed prevented the colours from being accurately rendered.

Mercenary contingents in English service evidently provided themselves with similar flags. A mercenary captain called Landenberg is recorded, in 1544, as having provided his men with standards of white and green with red crosses. Landenberg eventually fell out with Henry VIII's agents over the rates of pay which were to apply to his men;

consequently only the horsemen of his original contingent actually saw service with the English. Their standard included the royal arms, set in the centre of the cross of St George (see Plate H1).

When considering the developments outlined above, it is prudent to remember that heraldry was still very much a 'living' science in Henry VIII's day. Consider, for instance, the fate of Henry Howard, Earl of Surrey and one-time commander at Boulogne. In 1547 his enemies were able to precipitate his execution for high treason on the grounds that he had flaunted an ancient family claim to the throne by quartering the arms of Edward the Confessor with his own. His father, the Duke of Norfolk, was convicted of attempting to conceal his son's crime, and only avoided the headsman's axe because of the death of Henry VIII. It is also necessary to take into account the character of the king himself. As he grew older, Henry VIII became increasingly distrustful of the nobility and fearful of internal threats to his throne. Add to these factors Henry's ingrained dislike of 'livery and maintenance', and the form and timing of these changes in flags and uniforms are hardly surprising. They are just one facet of a general trend towards a concentration of authority in the hands of the king, at the expense of the aristocracy.

Further reading
The main primary sources referred to in this book are as follows:
Letters and Papers, Foreign and Domestic, of the Reign of Henry VIII, (particularly Vols 1, 3 pt1, 19, 20, 21 pt1); eds. J. Gairdner and R. H. Brodie.

This facsimile depicts one of the war-engines used in the 1544 campaign in France. It is probable that this type of machine is one of the 'shrympes' referred to in contemporary documents.

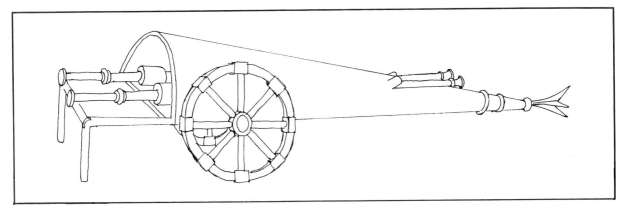

The union of the two noble and illustre families of York and Lancaster, Edward Hall, 1542 (generally known as Hall's Chronicle).

Secondary sources consist largely of myriad articles, or short references in long books. . . . For a complete list of such publications, the following bibliographies should be consulted:

A Bibliography of British Military History, ed. A. Bruce, 1981.

A Guide to the Sources of British Military History, ed. R. Highams, 1972.

For a general introduction to the subject and, indeed, to the period as a whole, Sir Charles Oman's *A History of the Art of War in the Sixteenth Century* (1937) is still useful and remains very readable. Finally, a special mention should be made of *Army Royal* by C. G. C. Cruickshank (1969); this is probably the best publication concerning Henry VIII's army. While specifically dealing with the French expedition of 1513, it draws on evidence from throughout the period.

The Plates

A: Flodden Field, 1513
A1: Billman
This man may be considered typical of the great mass of the English army at Flodden. His main weapon is a simple bill, an example of which survives in the Pitt Rivers Museum, Oxford. A rather elderly sword hangs at his waist, a relic of the preceding century. Over his plain countryman's garb he wears a jack. His head is protected by a 'kettle' hat, similar to one preserved in the Royal Armouries at the Tower of London.

A2: Archer of Sir Edward Stanley's contingent
One of the bowmen who contributed to the rout of the Highlanders, this man wears a 'base coat' of the Stanley livery colours, bearing the eagle claw badge of that family and the three crowns of the Bishopric of Ely (the bishop being Sir Edward's brother). At

This contemporary drawing shows an English army in action. Its regular formation is obviously idealised, but it is **interesting to note the prominence of various 'war-carts'. (British Library)**

his waist he carries a dagger of the 'balloch' type. On his wrist is a bracer of boiled leather, similar to that displayed in the British Museum. His rather unfashionable bonnet and sturdy boots with overstockings proclaim his rustic origins: he is perhaps a tenant farmer from the Stanleys' Lancashire estates.

A3: Soldier of the Earl of Surrey's contingent

A professional of Surrey's retinue, this man is more fashionably dressed than his provincial counterparts. Over his parti-coloured coat of white and green he wears breast and back plates, with a fauld but no tassets (based on a set preserved in Mendlesham Church, Suffolk). To protect his neck he wears a mail collar or 'standard'. On his head, a simple 'skull' is covered by a slashed and tabbed bonnet. His bill is of a slender, continental design, possibly an Italian import: the Royal Scottish Museum and the Wallace Collection both possess good examples. His short, single-edged sword is of a type preserved in the Royal Armouries.

B: The French Campaign, 1513

B1: Halberdier, Earl of Northumberland's guard

A detailed inventory exists of the Earl of Northumberland's equipage for the invasion of France. His 100-man guard were armed with halberds, this one of German manufacture. His armour is 'Almain rivet'. The arm defences are attached to his doublet by 'points' at the elbow. His hands are protected by extensions attached by a turning-pin to the 'splints' covering his forearms. A suit of this sort is preserved in the Westgate Museum, Winchester. He also wears a gorget and, on his head, a visored sallet of Italian manufacture (Wallace Collection). His sword is also made in Italy, although in the German style: an example survives in the Tower of London.

B2: Archer, Earl of Northumberland's contingent

The Earl's archers were also equipped with 'Almain rivet'. This man, however, is shown without his armour, displaying the coat supplied to men of this contingent. Captains were given coats of more expensive cloth, and did not wear the crescent badge of the Percy family seen here. His hat and quiver are both of the Percy livery colours. His secondary armament is a long 'rondel' dagger, still

popular in the early 16th century. This fine example is now to be seen at the Tower of London. He wears loose boots of soft leather, not often worn at this period except by travellers, huntsmen or soldiers.

B3: Captain, Earl of Northumberland's contingent

This man wears 'Almain rivet' of a rather superior quality. Based on a suit preserved in Mendlesham Church, Suffolk, it is fluted in the style then fashionable on far more expensive armours (particularly in Germany). He has discarded his sallet in favour of the yellow bonnet supplied to the captains and guardsmen of Northumberland's retinue. His dagger and Italian-made sword are

An English pikeman: this strangely clad figure was drawn during the 1540s. (British Library)

based on examples kept in the Tower of London. He carries the Percy family standard.

C1: Border Horseman

One of the light cavalrymen from the Northern Marches, who proved so valuable for scouting and skirmishing in France. He wears a cloth-covered brigandine with short mail sleeves; a simple sallet covers his head, while a bridle gauntlet protects his left hand. His kit is completed by a pair of long leather boots, rolled down at the top.

C2 & 3: Landsknechts

In stark contrast to the dress of Henry VIII's English troops is the gaudy attire of this pair of German hirelings. German fashions did influence

This painting depicts the meeting between Henry VIII and Maximilian I at Thérouanne. The two armoured halberdiers behind Henry's horse probably represent Yeomen of the Guard. In the background is a stylised representation of the Battle of the Spurs. (Reproduced by gracious permission of HM the Queen)

English styles at this period, but this kind of slashing of garments only surfaced in a diluted form. Most rank and file Landsknechts appear to have worn little armour at this time; one of these men, however, has equipped himself with a leather jerkin and a mantle of mail (based on an example in the Wallace Collection). The secondary armament of both men is the archetypal Landsknecht short-sword: the so-called *Katzbalger*.

D1: Yeoman of the Guard, circa 1520

This figure is taken from a bas-relief of Henry VIII's celebrated meeting with Francis I of France at the 'Field of the Cloth of Gold'. The colours of his coat are based on contemporary documents and eyewitness accounts. For the first half of Henry VIII's reign his guard were generally clothed in green and white (the Tudor livery colours) although the situation is complicated by the issue of several different coats for different purposes and degrees of formality. Bonnets and hose were not

uniform issue. This man carries a long-bow; alternatively he could have been armed with a halberd or javelins. In the field the Yeomen of the Guard appear to have worn half-armour (see the painting on page 44).

D2: Yeoman of the Guard, circa 1538
Red coats first came into use during the 1520s. At around the same time the rose began to be surmounted by a crown. This man is also based on a representation of the 'Field of the Cloth of Gold', but in this case the picture was painted in the late 1530s. This Yeoman wears what was probably the 'full dress' uniform of the latter years of Henry VIII's reign. Once again, only the coat was standard issue. His halberd is one of a set preserved in the Tower of London.

E1: English man-at-arms, circa 1540
Based on contemporary drawings, this gentleman is one of the few fully equipped English heavy cavalry available to Henry VIII. He wears armour of a German style, made circa 1530, topped by a close-helmet of a type peculiar to England and the Low Countries. His 'bastard' (hand-and-a-half) sword is of Italian manufacture. The horse is protected solely by a chanfron, although others in the same series of drawings are shown fully barded. His clothing and horse-trappings eschew personal heraldic motifs in favour of the cross of St George. (All his equipment is based on examples surviving in the Royal Armouries at the Tower of London.)

E2: Halberdier of the London Trained Bands, 1539
Lengthy descriptions survive of a grand muster of the London Trained Bands held in May 1539. A particularly detailed reference is made to the costume of the Lord Mayor's bodyguard of halberdiers, of whom this man is one. His clothes

A captain of foot, circa 1540. This man wears half-armour and a bonnet over his helmet. He carries a partizan. (British Library)

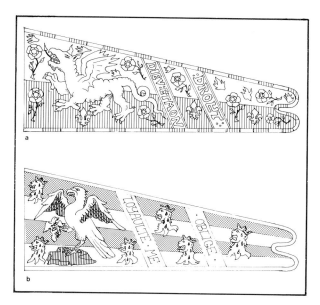

Standards: *(a) The King.* **Upper half: white. Lower half: green. Fringed green and white. Dragon: red. Sprinkled with gold fleurs-de-lys, red tongues of flame and Tudor roses.** *(b) The Duke of Suffolk.* **Striped red and white. Eagle: gold with blue wing feathers; it holds a golden bird and stands on a blue mound. Lions' heads: gold, sprinkled with blue 'tear-drops' and wearing red and white crowns. Both standards bore the cross of St George at the hoist.**

ape the Landsknecht style, with colourful linings pulled out through heavy slashing. The white and red reflect the colours of the City arms: Argent, a cross gules; in the first quarter a sword in pale, point upwards, of the last. (Rank and file members of the London Trained Bands bore these arms emblazoned on the front and back of white coats.) The cut of his leather jerkin is based on an example recovered from the wreck of the *Mary Rose*: it would have been laced up at the side.

F: The French Campaign, 1544
F1: Pikeman, Vanguard

This man wears the uniform of blue and red specified for the ward of the invasion army led by the Duke of Norfolk. Contemporary pictures appear to indicate that the uniform coat was generally worn over armour: this man sports a jack. His head is protected by a simple war-hat (Wallace Collection). His single-edged sword is of a type preserved in the Tower of London.

F2: Demilance

Typical of the bulk of the English gentry who served as cavalrymen, this man is protected by a suit of German light horseman's armour or *harnasch*. He

has put aside his helmet (probably a burgonet) in favour of a red bonnet: red appears to have been by far the most popular colour for military head-gear in England at this time. His hooded cloak, although not fashionable for civilian wear, is very practical for soldiering.

F3: Soldier of Thomas Caverden's contingent

Thomas Caverden was Master of the King's Tents. Contemporary documents show that he numbered among his retinue 50 men armed with 'sprinckyls', i.e. 'holy water sprinklers'—the example shown here is based on one displayed in the Tower of London. His head is protected by an early type of morion, also copied here from examples from the Royal Armouries. He wears the red and yellow colours of the main force 'Battle' of the invasion army.

G: The French Campaign, 1544
G1: Petty-captain of Foot

This figure is largely based on a contemporary drawing; however, his Italian-made burgonet and his partizan are both taken from examples preserved in the Tower of London. Apart from his helmet, he is afforded protection by a mail shirt (visible through his slashed coat) and mail strips attached to his sleeves. The *langue-de-bouef* type of partizan appears to have been the most popular foot officer's weapon in England at this date. Interestingly, many captains are also shown carrying shields of circular or oval shape, often strapped to their backs. To what extent these are the product of an artist's fancy is a matter of conjecture; they are, however, depicted in more than one source.

G2: Landsknecht captain

This man's fine suit of 'black and white' armour follows one preserved in the Wallace Collection; his sword is based on one in the Tower of London. By this date the Landsknecht sword had sprouted a knuckle-guard and a counter or ring-guard. He wields a boar-spear; like the *langue-de-boeuf* of his English counterpart, this was very much the mark of an officer of foot.

G3: Irish auxiliary

One of the 600 *Kern* taken to France for raiding and skirmishing; it is easy to imagine how such

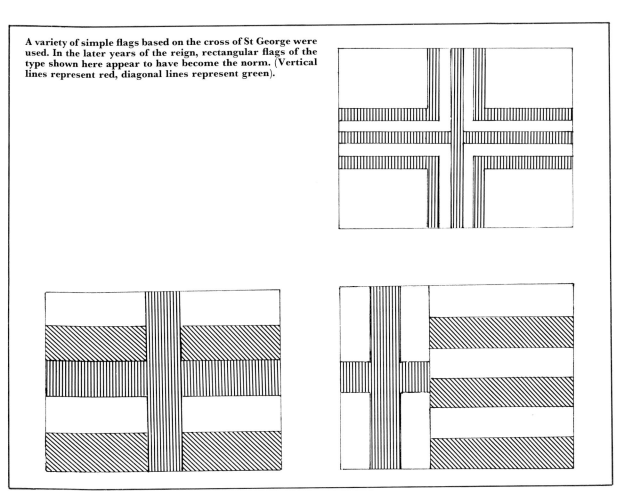

A variety of simple flags based on the cross of St George were used. In the later years of the reign, rectangular flags of the type shown here appear to have become the norm. (Vertical lines represent red, diagonal lines represent green).

outlandish troops would have appalled the French, especially given their penchant for collecting the severed heads of their foes. His tunic, dyed yellow with saffron, leaves, bark, salt and urine, is the quintessential Irish garment of this period. Over this, and a short doublet with hanging sleeves, he wears his 'Erse mantle': an extremely practical rough cloak which could also be used for bedding. His hair falls over his eyes in a *glib*—a style assiduously cultivated by most Irishmen at this time. *Kern* were primarily armed with javelins (some are shown with flights, like present-day darts). This man also carries a sword of peculiarly Irish design, based on an excavated example. These weapons are invariably shown held in the hand or tucked under the arm, rather than suspended from a belt.

H: The French Campaign, 1544
H1: German cavalryman
An example of the mercenary horsemen hired by

Henry VIII to eke out the meagre cavalry strength of the English army. This man is a true heavy cavalryman, rather than a pistoleer of the *reiter* type. He wears a full suit of plate, based on an example which features in the Wallace Collection. At his side is a bastard sword of German manufacture (Royal Armouries). He bears the standard carried by the horsemen of a contingent raised by the mercenary captain Landenberg.

H2: Arquebusier
Another figure based on the drawings in the British Library Manuscript Augustus III.a. (see also Plates E1 and G1). Arquebusiers were scarce in England; consequently this man is likely to be another of Henry VIII's foreign hirelings—probably Italian or Spanish. The arquebus is based on a similar weapon in the Tower of London. Also prominent are his box-like powder flask and the match wound around his forearm.

Notes sur les planches en couleur

A1 Ce soldat qui caractérise la majorité des soldats anglais à *Flodden* porte une simple hallebarde (*bill*) et une épée démontée; il a passé sur de simples vêtements de paysan, une jaque (*jack*) ouatée et un casque *kettle*. **A2** Notez la livrée (*livery coat*) aux couleurs de la famille Stanley, avec l'écusson à serre d'aigle de cette famille et les trois couronnes de l'évêché de la famille d'*Ely*. Son costume suggère qu'il s'agit d'un fermier à bail du domaine de la famille Stanley. **A3** Un soldat professionnel au costume plus élégant, son armure et ses armes sont basées ici sur des exemples qui ont été préservés: une cuirasse à plates couvrant le dos et la poitrine, un col de mailles ou *standard* et sous son bonnetune coiffe métallique; une hallebade (*bill*) plus fine, peut-être une importation italienne et une épée à un seul tranchant.

B1 Un inventaire détaillé qui a survécu permet une reconstruction presque complète. C'est le type d'armure acheté en large quantité pour l'infanterie lourde et appelée en Angleterre *Almain rivet*. **B2** Les archers de ce contingent recevainet aussi l'armure *Almain rivet*, quoique cet homme soit préservé sans la sienne afin de montrer le manteau avec l'écusson et la famille Percy; les couleurs du bonnet et du carquois sont celles de la livrée de la famille *Percy*. **B3** Armure de meilleure qualité, rainurée selon le style allemand; il a abandonné son casque *salade* (sallet) au profit du bonnet jaune porté par les officiers et les soldats de la Garde de la suite de Northumberland. Il porte l'étendard de la famille *Percy*.

C1 Les soldats de la redoutable cavalerie légère de la frontière anglo-écossaise portaient des cottes de mailles, des brigandines, de simples casques et souvent une protection pour la main gauche qui tenait la bride. **C2, C3** Soldats allemands loués vêtus de clinquant dans des vêtements à taillades; l'on voyait peu d'armures, mais l'un d'eux porte une cape de mailles sur son pourpoint de cuir.

D1 D'après un bas-relief de l'entrevue de Henry VIII avec François Ier au 'Camp du Drap d'or', couleurs d'après des documents et récits contemporains. L'on porta pendant la première moitié du règne de Henry VIII les couleurs de la livrée *Tudor*, blanc et vert; les bonnets et chausses n'étaient pas distribués. **D2** Des manteaux rouges furent utilisés à compter des années 1520 alors que le symbole de la couronne apparut au-dessus de la rose ds Tudors. Ce soldat est reconstitué d'après un tableau des années 1530 présentant probablement la 'tenue complète' de la dernière partie du règne. Les soldats de la Garde portaient sur le champ de bataille une demi-armure.

E1 Armure de modèle allemand, env. 1530, portée par l'un des quelques cavaliers anglais de Henry VIII à être revêtus d'une armure lourde; le casque est caractéristique de l'Angleterre et des Pays Bas. **E2** Une description détaillée de la Garde du Corps de hallebardiers du lord maire a permis cette reconstitution. Notez les styles du *Landsknecht*; le pourpoint de cuir est basé sur un exemple trouvé dans l'épave de la *Mary Rose*.

F1 Cet uniforme bleu et blanc était d'usage de porter le manteau au-dessus de l'armmure; cet homme porte une jaque (*jack*). **F2** Il semble que la plus grande partie de la petite noblesse anglaise qui servait dans la cavalerie ait porté une armure légère de cavalier, ou *harnasch*, de type allemand. **F3** Le gros de la troupe—*Battle*—portait du rouge et jaune. 50 hommes de cette garde officielle portaient l'aspergès' (holy water sprinkler) ou fléau à pointe. Notez le premier modèle de casque *morion*.

G1 D'après un dessin contemporain avec *bourguignonne* (burgonet) et *partizan* italiens, copiés sur des exemples qui ont été préservés. Notez la chemise de mailles que l'on peut voir à travers le manteau à taillades et les bandes de mailles sur les bras. Ce modèle *langue-de-boeuf* de *partizan* était une arme populaire chez les officiers. L'on a souvent montré les capitaines avec de petits boucliers ronds ou ovals, souvent attachés au dos avec une courroie. **G2** Un bel ensemble d'armure 'blanche et noire' prélevé sur un spécimen préservé; notez l'épieu, une autre arme populaire auprès des officiers. **G3** Le *kern* irlandais, dans une tunique couleur saffran caractéristique, le lourd manteau et la coiffure irlandaise. Armés de javelots (dont certains avec portée comme les fléchettes) et d'épées comme celle montrée sur cette illustration, ces barbares étaient employés pour les attaques; même à cette date, c'étaient toujours des chasseurs de têtes.

H1 Soldats de la cavalerie avec armure complète, du genre loués pour renflouer la faible cavalerie anglaise; l'étendard est celui porté par la compagnie du capitaine mercenaire Landenberg. **H2** Un mercenaire probablement italien ou espagnol, dessiné ici d'après un manuscript contemporain, son arme et sa flasque à poudre étant des exemples qui ont été préservés.

Farbtafeln

A1 Typisch für die Mehrheit der englischen Soldaten bei Flodden sind die einfachen 'bill' (Hellebarde) und das altmodische Schwert; über der einfachen Bauernbekleidung eine gesteppte Jacke ('jack') und ein 'kettle'-Helm. **A2** Man beachte den 'livery coat' in Stanleys Farben, mit dem Adlerklauenwappen der Familie und den drei Kronen des Familienbischofssitzes Ely. Das Kostüm lässt auf einen Bauern des Stanleyschen Landguts schliessen. **A3** Ein modisch gekleideter Berufssoldat; Panzer und Waffen nach erhalten gebliebenen Exemplaren: Kürass mit Brust- und Rückenpanzer, Kettenkragen ('standard') und unter der Haube eine metallene Kopfbedeckung; eine schmale 'bill', möglicherweise aus Italien importiert, und ein einschneidiges Schwert.

B1 Ein erhalten gebliebenes detailliertes Inventarium erlaubt eine weitgehend vollständige Rekonstruktion. Diese Art Panzer wurde in grossen Mengen für die schwerze Infanterie angeschafft, in England als 'Almain rivet' bezeichnet. **B2** Bogenschützen dieses Kontingents erhielten ebenfalls 'Almain rivet'; dieser Mann stellt dagegen seinen Rock mit dem Familienwappen der Percys zur Schau; Hut und Köcher haben die Livreefarben der Percys. **B3** Hochwertiger Panzer, im deutschen Stil kanneliert; der 'sallet'-Helm ist durch die gelbe Kappe ersetzt, die von Offizieren und Gardisten im Gefolge der Familie Northumberland getragen wurde. Er trägt das Familienbanner der Percys.

C1 Die grimmige leichte Kavallerie an der englisch-schotti-schen Grenze trug Kettenpanzer, Panzerhemd, einfache Helme und häufig auch einen Schutz für die Zügelhand. **C2, C3** Bunt gekleidete deutsche Söldner in geschlitztem Kostüm; wenige Waffen, aber einer der Männer trägt einen Kettenpanzerumhang über der Lederweste.

D1 Nach einem Halbrelief mit dem Zusammentreffen von Heinrich VIII. und Franz I. auf dem 'Camp du Drap d'Or' (Farben nach zeitgenössischen Dokumenten und Berichten). Während der ersten Hälfte von Heinrichs Regierungszeit trug die Livree des Hauses Tudor die Farben weiss und grün; Kappen und Kniehosen wurden nicht ausgegeben. **D2** Rote Röcke wurden seit den 1520er Jahren benutzt; das Kronabzeichen erschien über der Tudor-Rose. Diese Figur stammt aus einem Gemälde der 1530er Jahre und trägt wahrscheinlich das volle Kostüm aus der Spätzeit von Heinrichs Regierung. Auf dem Schlachtfeld trugen Gardisten einen Halbpanzer.

E1 Rüstung im deutschen Stil, ca. 1530, von einem der wenigen Mitglieder von Heinrichs schwer bewaffneter Kavallerie getragen; der Helm ist typisch für England und die Niederlande. **E2** Eine detaillierte zeitgenössische Beschreibung des Hellebardiers im Leibdienst des Londoner Oberbürgermeisters ('Lord Mayor') ermöglichte diese Rekonstruktion; man beachte die Imitation des Landsknecht-Stils. Die Lederweste nach einem an Bord der 'Mary Rose' gefundenen Exemplar.

F1 Die blau/rote Uniform war eigens für die vorderen Reihen der vom Herzog von Norfolk geführten Invasionsarmee entworfen. Zeitgenössische Bilder weisen darauf hin, dass über der Rüstung ein Mantel getragen wurde; dieser Mann trägt die kurze 'jack'. **F2** Rüstung ('harnasch'), für leicht bewaffnete Berittene nach dem deutschen Typ, typisch für die meisten englischen Landadligen, die in der Kavallerie dienten. **F3** Der Hauptteil des Heers ('Battle') trug die Farben rot und gelb. Der mit Stacheln versehene Dreschflegel ('Weihwassersprenger') wurde über 50 Mitgliedern dieser Offiziersgarde mitgeführt. Man beachte die Frühform des 'moriot'-Helms.

G1 Nach einer zeitgenössischen Zeichnung; mit italienischem 'burgonet' und 'partizan' nach erhaltenen Exemplaren. Man beachte das Kettenhemd, erkennbar durch die geschlitzte Kleidung, und die Kettenstreifen auf den Armen. Dieser 'langue-de-boeuf' 'partizan' war eine bei Offizieren populäre Waffe. Hauptmannsgrade werden häufiger mit runden oder ovalen Schilden abgebildet, die oft am Rücken festgeschnürt sind. **G2** Eine gut erhaltene Rüstung in schwarz/weiss; man beachte den Sauspiess, ebenfalls beliebt bei Offizieren. **G3** Der irische 'kern', typischer safrangelber Rock, schwerer Mantel und irische Frisur. Bewaffnet mit kurzen Wurfspiessen ('javelins') oder Wurfpfeilen ('flights') diese barbarischen Krieger wurden bei Plünderungen eingesetzt und waren noch zu diesem Zeitpunkt Kopfjäger.

H1 Ein voll gerüsteter Kavallerist vom Typ der zur Verstärkung der schwachen englischen Kavallerie angeworbenen Männer. Die Standarte gehört zur Kompanie der Söldnerhauptmanns Landenberg. **H2** Wahrscheinlich ein italienischer oder spanischer Söldner, nach einer zeitgenössischen Handschrift gezeichnet; Waffe und Pulverdose nach erhaltenen Exemplaren.